MW00675155

THIS STUDY ABROAD JOURNAL IS THE PROPERTY OF

EMAIL:

REWARD:

PROGRAM NAME

VISA DEADLINE

SCHOLARSHIP DEADLINE

PRE-DEPARTURE ORIENTATION

OUTBOUND FLIGHT

ON-SITE ORIENTATION

PROGRAM BREAK

ON-CAMPUS COURSE SELECTION

ON-CAMPUS HOUSING DEADLINE

FINAL EXAMS

FLIGHT HOME

Connect with us!
Use #abroadjournal and share how you're using your Journal!

@theabroadjournal   /abroadjournal   @abroad_journal

The
STUDY ABROAD
Journal

Your roadmap to an epic study abroad experience

Created by
Natalie Garrett & Brooke Roberts

BRNG
CREATIVE

Published by BRNG Creative LLC
ISBN 978-0-9980855-0-0

Brooke Roberts and Natalie Garrett

All rights reserved.

© 2016 Natalie Garrett & Brooke Roberts. All rights reserved.

Design by Blair Stapp | www.blairstapp.com

All material in this book may not be reproduced, transmitted, or distributed in any form without the written permission of the authors or BRNG Creative LLC.

For information about permission to reproduce selections from this book, email **hello@thestudyabroadjournal.com**.

Visit our website at **www.thestudyabroadjournal.com**.

PUBLISHER'S DISCLAIMER

While the publisher and authors have used their best efforts in preparing this journal, they make no representations or warranties with respect to the accuracy or completeness of the contents of this journal. The advice and strategies contained herein may not be suitable for your situation. You should consult a professional where appropriate. Neither the publisher nor authors shall be liable for any loss of profit or any other commercial damages, including but not limited to special, incidental, consequential, or other damages.

DEDICATION

For all the students out there who have the audacity and courage to study abroad ... and make it an epic experience.

This is for you.

Seven reasons this journal will rock your study abroad

1 **Collect your memories in one place.**

When you study abroad, you might be sharing elements of your experience across multiple platforms, social media channels, and with different audiences. The Study Abroad Journal is for you to capture all your thoughts, goals, reflections, and experiences in one place. You'll walk away with a beautiful keepsake that you can return to again and again.

2 **Measure the value of your program.**

Study abroad ain't cheap. This Journal gives you the power to design a powerful study abroad experience that will pay out huge dividends (this is called ROI or Return on Investment). If you follow our plan, you'll have tangible, measurable knowledge, skills, and experience to leverage in your future career.

3 **Track your progress toward your goals.**

Study abroad is about having a great time, learning a lot, and evolving as a global citizen. But it's hard to see how far you've come if you don't track as you go. The Journal will help you understand where you want to go, how to get there, and keep you on track.

4 **Prove you did something besides (just) party.**

Hey, we know you're going to have a fun time. You absolutely should! But students often struggle to show that they did much more than "have a good time." The Study Abroad Journal will help you dive deeper into your experience and walk away with some fun memories and some tangible, super impressive learning outcomes as well.

5 **Own your experience.**

While your program may have been planned by someone else, you have the power to make your experience meaningful. Your Journal will help you explain what you learned, how you grew, and what skills you will carry to your next adventure and your future career. All designed by you.

6 **Get focused on what you REALLY want.**

What do you want to say you did/accomplished when you return? How will you impress future employers, grad school admissions officers, or even mom and dad? We're all about reverse-engineering your study abroad program so you can stay focused on what is important to you. First, you'll zero in on your end goals, then you'll make a plan for how to get there.

7 **Take your experience from awesome to epic.**

Most study abroad students come home and say "it was awesome!" and they can't seem to tease out why. Your Journal will help you tease out the value of your experience and articulate it in a meaningful way to your parents, professors, friends, future employers, and perhaps some future dates.

66

By recording your dreams and goals on paper, you set in motion the process of becoming the person you most want to be. Put your future in good hands— your own.

99

—**Mark Victor Hansen**

CONTENTS

HOW TO REACH ME

(Tear out this page and give it to someone you care about.)

Dear Loved One,

Thank you so much for all the amazing support and encouragement you've provided to me as I plan and now depart for this experience abroad.

I'm so excited to see how this experience changes and challenges me.

Because I want to get the most out of this experience, I want to focus on where I'm at, who I'm with, and what I'm doing on location as much as possible.

We may not communicate as much as we normally do, but don't worry, I won't forget you. ;)

Here are the places I'll be posting about my experience
(insert social media profile handles, blog URLs, etc.)

....

....

....

And here's how I'd love to stay in touch while I'm abroad
(many of these services have apps you can download to your phone):

SKYPE

WHATSAPP ....

VIBER ....

GOOGLE VOICE ....

FACETIME ....

TEAR HERE

" It always seems impossible until it's done. "

—Nelson Mandela

WHY

It's difficult to know where to start goal-setting for an experience you haven't EXPERIENCED yet. Blank pages in a brand new travel journal can be daunting and sometimes a little structure to get the ball rolling is just what you need.

This Study Abroad Journal is your roadmap to an epic experience abroad.

As you know, study abroad isn't cheap and you deserve to get the most out of your experience. This doesn't mean that you should go "full diva" on the hard-working people administering your program. What it DOES mean is that you take ownership of your own success. The Study Abroad Journal ensures that you set goals and intentions, build a roadmap to meet those goals, and take some time to thoughtfully document and reflect on it all.

Additionally, most study abroad alumni struggle to articulate the value of their experience and the skills they developed during their program. It's not just about including a line on your resume—it's about sharing the context, nuance, and depth of your experience as it relates to the work you want to do in the future.

Finally, it is hard to see how far you've come if you don't know where you started. Keeping a journal while you're abroad will give you a reason to celebrate when you've blasted through all your action plans, met your goals, and you're reflecting on what an amazing experience YOU created.

Let's face it, we don't use pen and paper enough anymore. There's something romantic about having a physical journal to carry with you throughout your experience.

Let's face it, we don't use pen and paper enough anymore. There's something romantic about having a physical journal to carry with you throughout your experience. Your grandkids will think it's awesome, too.

If you're doing a 'traditional' study abroad experience, you may not know it, but there's a whole team of people building your experience behind the scenes. Someone is finding housing, enrolling you in travel insurance, making sure your credits transfer, and the list goes on...

These are all logistics, but the experience of study abroad can be so much more.

We created the The Study Abroad Journal to help you move beyond logistics, country-hopping, and saying it was "awesome." Although you may have a very well-planned program ahead of you, it's you, the participant, who has the most control over making your experience a powerful part of your academic program, your career growth, and your personal development.

The power to create an incredible study abroad experience is now in your hands.

WHO

We (Brooke and Natalie) co-created this journal after participating in six study abroad experiences of our own, guiding thousands of students through THEIR study abroad programs around the world, and also launching a few travel and study abroad companies.

We are professionals in the field of education abroad and entrepreneurs who have mastered the art of goal-setting and getting sh*t done. In The Study Abroad Journal, you will find our proven practices of goal setting, strategic action planning, and reflection that we've used in our academic and professional lives to achieve our goals.

Enough about us, let's get on to the business of rocking your study abroad experience!

Begin with the end in mind.

Just saying you studied abroad WON'T impress anyone. What you *accomplish* during your experience WILL impress everyone.

You'll start with the big goals you want to achieve by the end of your program and then fill in smaller actions items for each day, week, and month that help you achieve those big goals. We will walk you through step-by-step in the beginning and then, you'll be off achieving your goals like a champ!

Let's do this...

EPIC

study abroad experiences don't just

happen.

They start with a

solid plan of **ACTION,**

consistent **REVIEW,**

and a *curious mind.*

It's up to **YOU**

to make some *magic* happen

during your time abroad.

The **Study Abroad Journal** is your

ROADMAP.
You can do it.

THE FRAMEWORK

We've outlined four key areas of focus for your journal. Keep these or create your own. As long as your areas of focus are exciting to you, we're in full support!

Academic Engagement

Academic Engagement activities help you dive deeper into your course of study and understand it from a cross-cultural perspective. Do they approach finance differently in Asia? How is art history explored in Latin America? Maybe the actual academic philosophy of your university abroad is different than your home country and you want to explore how that country's history of higher education philosophy evolved. **Academic Engagement** goals should help you seek out fun and engaging learning opportunities to explore your field of study in your host country.

Cultural Exploration

The decision to study abroad typically starts with a natural curiosity about a country, the culture, the language, food, people, history, and more. **Cultural Exploration** activities get you into the local community to help you understand more about the inner workings of a society. Of course, you'll get some cultural discovery in your courses, but your Journal will help you to dive even deeper. Whatever gets you excited, we'll give you ideas on how to explore the culture through different lenses.

Career Development

This is the area where you can make your journal and your time abroad really **work for YOU**. By getting clear on your career-related goals, you will walk away with tangible skills, knowledge, experiences, and connections to help you land an internship or your first job after college. Maybe you'll set a goal to grow your professional network in your host city or explore the different career options available locally. Being diligent in this quadrant is the key to come away with a solid professional foundation to propel your career forward.

Wild Card

Academic Engagement, Cultural Exploration, and Career Development are all 'inside the box' areas of focus that are extremely important to carving out a well-rounded, dynamic study abroad experience. **Wild Card** goals are the opposite and have zero boundaries. Your WC goals (not to be confused with 'water closet') may be related to academics, career, or cultural exploration, or they might not. Get creative about what is possible with your own WC goals. Maybe you want to run a marathon abroad or you're really into punk bands and you want to explore the local punk scene. Whatever it is, carve out the time to focus on the things that matter most to you. Like a water closet, this is the place where you get sh*t done. (Yeah, we went there.)

STRUCTURE

1. Brainstorm & Dream

2. Set Realistic Goals

3. Make an Action Plan

4. Assess

5. Reflect

Within each area, you'll find 5 steps to make your journal work for you. When you **Brainstorm and Dream**, imagine what's possible in a world without limitations. However, since you are studying abroad in the real world (which has a few limitations like time, gravity, program schedules), you'll move from brainstorming to setting **Realistic Goals**.

After you've set a program goal in each area, you'll **make an Action Plan** to help you meet those goals. An 'action plan' isn't a 'to-do' list. YOU get to decide what to include. *If you dread it, don't add it.*

Next you'll answer the foundational question: How did it go? You'll **Assess** whether you made progress towards your goals, **Reflect** on your action items, then decide how to move forward. Make sure you celebrate your success along the way! You've earned it.

It's your choice: Stick to the structure we've provided by setting a program goal for each area (AE, CE, CD, & WC) or grab the closest blunt object, scratch them all out and make your own. Make sure everything that goes into this journal is something that's important to YOU.

Use our framework and structure as inspiration to set goals that are unique to you!

YOUR STUDY ABROAD JOURNAL

Tying it all together

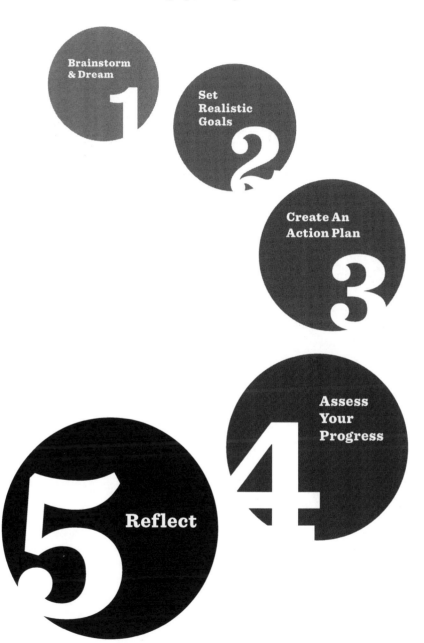

IN REAL LIFE

To help you see how this might play out, we've created an IRL example to show you exactly how our framework can be applied in a practical way.

We'll walk you through a Career Development goal and how the Brainstorming, Goal Setting, and Action Planning might look if you were an accounting major studying in London.

Brainstorming

— Meet the CEO of a major Accounting firm
— Get a job offer to work at a big 5 accounting firm in Europe
— Find a paid internship in London for the summer after my program
— Create a young accountants networking group for Expats

More awesome+ridiculous ideas here....

You see how a lot of these ideas are really big, may be unrealistic, or take a lot of work to accomplish? It's all "doable" but maybe not realistic. Now it's time to synthesize it down into one manageable goal that you could achieve.

Goal Setting

— **Goal:** Grow my professional network in the corporate accounting industry in London

Based on all the **BIG** ideas we had for ourselves in the Brainstorm stage, do you see how this particular goal seems manageable and may actually lead to one of the outcomes you've dreamt about? It's measurable, specific, and has a clear target you can try to hit. Now it's time to map out exactly how you're going to do it.

Action Planning

1. Land 10 informational interviews with current corporate accountants
2. Attend 3 networking events for accounting professionals
3. Find 2 accounting/business related workshops/seminars to attend
4. Ask for introductions to local accounting professionals from my network
5. Create a business card and have printed - Moo.com is great!
6. Attend a local alumni reception for my college/university

GOAL IDEAS

Here's are some Program Goal ideas to help you start brainstorming your own.

AE Academic Engagement

- Understand the study of art history compared to another country
- Identify 3 themes in local political views about climate change
- Create an annotated bibliography of the recent research in my local country on sports medicine
- Learn the educational path of a faculty member in my field who I admire

CE Cultural Exploration

- Identify your favorite local dish in the region and learn the recipe
- What is the history of my host country through the eyes of my own country and how does it compare to that of my host country?
- Have an everyday conversation in the local language for 60 minutes without pausing

CD Career Development

- Grow my network in my field of study
- Learn how to do video editing
- Gain experience in my industry through volunteer, intern, or paid experiences
- Teach myself the top three software systems used in my industry
- Create a one-page resume JUST using my study abroad experiences

WC Wild Card

- Explore the punk band scene in my host city and write about how it differs from the scene back home
- Complete a local running race and use the training runs to learn more about my city
- Blog about the local fashion I see everyday on my way to class

Need more ideas? *Visit http://thestudyabroadjournal.com/ideas*

Make The Study Abroad Journal work for you. *You've got the background, you know how and why The Study Abroad Journal can work for you, so now it's time to DIVE IN and do the work!*

BRAINSTORM YOUR PROGRAM GOALS

The first rule of brainstorming is that there are no rules. Think about all the different things you want to learn, do, see, and experience during your program. There's no judgment, no wrong answers, no grade. Start brainstorming, then leave it for 24 hours, and come back with fresh eyes and ideas.

You are a superhero and can DO IT ALL.

 Academic Engagement

What kind of things do you want to experience related to your field of study? What do you want to see, study, read, do, etc?

BRAINSTORM YOUR PROGRAM GOALS

 Cultural Exploration

How do you want to engage with the local culture? Sites you want to see, food you want to taste, sounds you want to hear, etc.?

Career Development

How do you want to impress future hiring managers with your study abroad experience? What do you want to be able to say that you learned? What skills would you like to develop? Who do you want to meet?

 **Wild Card**

Think about your passions. What would you love to explore that's outside of the traditional areas of school, work, and culture? You could also add a goal to really rock one of the other areas.

Once you've done some dreaming, take a look at everything you wrote. What themes emerge? What ideas get you the most excited? Now it's time to start making a plan....

SET YOUR PROGRAM GOALS

Now that you've brainstormed all the different goals and things you could achieve during your study abroad experience (if you were a superhero), it's time to narrow them down and focus on one goal per area - that's four goals during your entire program. One goal per area may not sound like a lot, but remember that each goal will be your north star.

How you set program goals will depend on YOUR program length, structure, and schedule and should be attainable while also taking advantage of everything your program has to offer.

Your Study Abroad Journal should enhance your program, not take it over.

AE **Academic Engagement**

CE **Cultural Exploration**

CD **Career Development**

WC **Wild Card**

Next, you'll break each goal down into monthly, weekly, and daily action items.

PROGRAM ACTIONS

Take each of your program goals and outline 3-5 key action items to achieve that larger program goal. As you plan each month and week of your program, you'll break each action item into smaller tasks.

Break down each of your goals into bite-sized, **REALISTIC** action items that you can conceivably do nearly every day of your program.

Actions need to be measurable and something you can plot on a calendar (hint... next up, you'll find five monthly calendars).

AE Academic Engagement

Goal:

1.
2.
3.
4.
5.

CE Cultural Exploration

Goal:

1.
2.
3.
4.
5.

CD Career Development

Goal:

1.
2.
3.
4.
5.

WC Wild Card

Goal:

1.
2.
3.
4.
5.

MONTH

START HERE ▶

It's time to plan the month ahead! What two action items will you accomplish this month towards each of your program goals? Outline them on the right and plot them on the calendar below.

GOLD STAR MOMENT	SUNDAY	MONDAY	TUESDAY
In future months, you'll review last month and give yourself a gold star for actions you completed towards each goal. Try to earn 5 gold stars for each area. (This $&%^ ain't easy, so be generous with those stars.)			
ACADEMIC ENGAGEMENT ○ ○ ○ ○ ○ **CULTURAL EXPLORATION** ○ ○ ○ ○ ○ **CAREER DEVELOPMENT** ○ ○ ○ ○ ○ **WILD CARD** ○ ○ ○ ○ ○			
"Travel makes one modest. You see what a tiny place you occupy in the world." —Gustave Flaubert			

AE
1. ....
2.

CE
1. ....
2.

CD
1. ....
2.

WC
1. ....
2.

WEDNESDAY	THURSDAY	FRIDAY	SATURDAY

START HERE ▶

On the right, outline a couple of action items for each of your goals that you'll tackle this month. Then plot those action items on the calendar below.

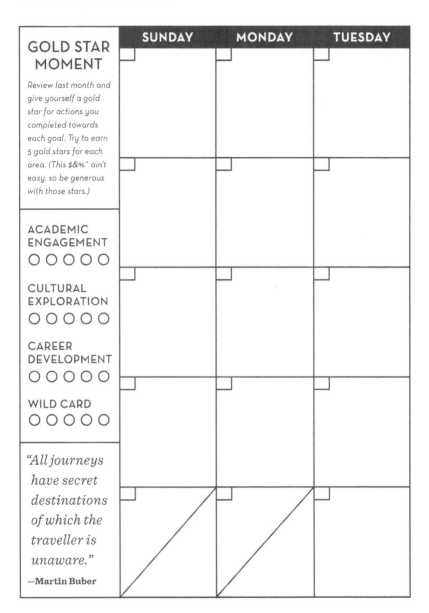

GOLD STAR MOMENT

Review last month and give yourself a gold star for actions you completed towards each goal. Try to earn 5 gold stars for each area. (This $&%^ ain't easy, so be generous with those stars.)

ACADEMIC ENGAGEMENT
○ ○ ○ ○ ○

CULTURAL EXPLORATION
○ ○ ○ ○ ○

CAREER DEVELOPMENT
○ ○ ○ ○ ○

WILD CARD
○ ○ ○ ○ ○

"All journeys have secret destinations of which the traveller is unaware."
—**Martin Buber**

SUNDAY	MONDAY	TUESDAY

AE 1. _____
2.

CE 1. _____
2.

CD 1. _____
2.

WC 1. _____
2.

WEDNESDAY	THURSDAY	FRIDAY	SATURDAY

MONTH ....

START HERE ▶

On the right, outline a couple of action items for each of your goals that you'll tackle this month. Then plot those action items on the calendar below.

	SUNDAY	MONDAY	TUESDAY
GOLD STAR MOMENT *Review last month and give yourself a gold star for actions you completed towards each goal. Try to earn 5 gold stars for each area. (This $&%^ ain't easy, so be generous with those stars.)*			
ACADEMIC ENGAGEMENT ○ ○ ○ ○ ○ **CULTURAL EXPLORATION** ○ ○ ○ ○ ○ **CAREER DEVELOPMENT** ○ ○ ○ ○ ○ **WILD CARD** ○ ○ ○ ○ ○			
"Travelling— it leaves you speechless, then turns you into a storyteller." **—Ibn Battuta**			

AE 1. ....
    2.

CE 1. ....
    2.

CD 1. ....
    2.

WC 1. ....
    2.

WEDNESDAY	THURSDAY	FRIDAY	SATURDAY

MONTH ....

START HERE ▶

On the right, outline a couple of action items for each of your goals that you'll tackle this month. Then plot those action items on the calendar below.

GOLD STAR MOMENT	SUNDAY	MONDAY	TUESDAY
Review last month and give yourself a gold star for actions you completed towards each goal. Try to earn 5 gold stars for each area. (This $&%^ ain't easy, so be generous with those stars.)			
ACADEMIC ENGAGEMENT ○ ○ ○ ○ ○			
CULTURAL EXPLORATION ○ ○ ○ ○ ○ **CAREER DEVELOPMENT** ○ ○ ○ ○ ○			
WILD CARD ○ ○ ○ ○ ○			
"Better to see something once, than to hear about it a thousand times." —**Asian Proverb**			

WEDNESDAY	THURSDAY	FRIDAY	SATURDAY

MONTH

START HERE ▶

On the right, outline a couple of action items for each of your goals that you'll tackle this month. Then plot those action items on the calendar below.

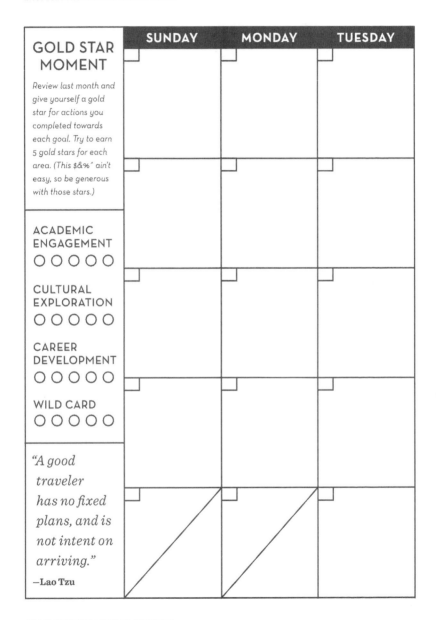

GOLD STAR MOMENT

Review last month and give yourself a gold star for actions you completed towards each goal. Try to earn 5 gold stars for each area. (This $&%^ ain't easy, so be generous with those stars.)

ACADEMIC ENGAGEMENT
○ ○ ○ ○ ○

CULTURAL EXPLORATION
○ ○ ○ ○ ○

CAREER DEVELOPMENT
○ ○ ○ ○ ○

WILD CARD
○ ○ ○ ○ ○

"A good traveler has no fixed plans, and is not intent on arriving."
—Lao Tzu

SUNDAY	MONDAY	TUESDAY

AE
1. _____
2.

CE
1. _____
2.

CD
1. _____
2.

WC
1. _____
2.

WEDNESDAY	THURSDAY	FRIDAY	SATURDAY

"

Not I, nor anyone else can travel that road for you.

You must travel it by yourself.

It is not far. It is within reach.

Perhaps you have been on it since you were born, and did not know. Perhaps it is everywhere— on water and land.

"

—**Walt Whitman**

———— • ———— • ————

DATE

*I never travel without my diary. One should always
have something sensational to read in the train.*

— Oscar Wilde

Good morning!

WHAT ARE YOU MOST GRATEFUL FOR TODAY?

What's on the agenda for today?

① ....

② ....

③ ....

Good evening!
What will you remember most about today?

....

....

....

What actions did you take to meet your goals today?

....

....

....

*I'm not running away from anything. I'm
running towards everything I've ever wanted.*

— Maria Maslin

Good morning!

WHAT ARE YOU MOST GRATEFUL FOR TODAY?

What's on the agenda for today?

1.
2.
3.

Good evening!
What will you remember most about today?

What actions did you take to meet your goals today?

—— • —— • ——
DATE

Just as a painter paints, and a ponderer ponders,
a writer writes, and a wanderer wanders.

— *Roman Payne*

Good morning!

WHAT ARE YOU MOST GRATEFUL FOR TODAY?

What's on the agenda for today?

① ....
② ....
③ ....

Good evening!
What will you remember most about today?

....
....
....

What actions did you take to meet your goals today?

....
....
....

*The real voyage of discovery consists not in
seeking new landscapes, but in having new eyes.*

— Marcel Proust

Good morning!

WHAT ARE YOU MOST GRATEFUL FOR TODAY?

What's on the agenda for today?

1.
2.
3.

Good evening!
What will you remember most about today?

What actions did you take to meet your goals today?

———— • ———— • ————

DATE

*We would oppose the turning of the planet
and refuse the setting of the sun.*

— Dave Eggers

Good morning!

WHAT ARE YOU MOST GRATEFUL FOR TODAY?

What's on the agenda for today?

1. _____
2. _____
3. _____

Good evening!
What will you remember most about today?

_____
_____
_____

What actions did you take to meet your goals today?

_____
_____
_____

*What gives value to travel is fear. It breaks
down a kind of inner structure we all have.*

— Elizabeth Benedict

Good morning!

WHAT ARE YOU MOST GRATEFUL FOR TODAY?

What's on the agenda for today?

1.
2.
3.

Good evening!
What will you remember most about today?

What actions did you take to meet your goals today?

DATE

Live, travel, adventure, bless,
and don't be sorry.

— Jack Kerouac

Good morning!

WHAT ARE YOU MOST GRATEFUL FOR TODAY?

What's on the agenda for today?

1. _____
2. _____
3. _____

Good evening!
What will you remember most about today?

_____
_____
_____

What actions did you take to meet your goals today?

_____
_____
_____

THOUGHTS & REFLECTIONS

You made it through your first week! *How'd it go?*

Time to Assess

You just finished the very first week of your study abroad experience. Time to review how things are going so far. Have you made progress on your goals? What are you discovering from your efforts so far? How do you need to adjust your goals and your action items moving forward? Have you been so busy settling in that you forgot about your goals?

It will take some time to get into a rhythm and learn what REALISTIC goals and action items mean for you.

Assessing is less about saying, 'Done! I checked this off my list!' and more about saying, 'Hmmm... I blew that out of the water, how can I challenge myself next month?' or 'Wow. That goal was TOO big. I see that I need to regroup and be more realistic next month.' OR (especially in your first weeks) 'My #1 goal is to settle in and get comfortable in my new surroundings.'

Especially in your first weeks, take the opportunity to assess each of your goals and revise them.

We want you to achieve your program goals, so make them realistic!

WEEKLY REFLECTION //

What amazing things happened this week?

What will you remember most about this week?

What goals did you work toward this week?

What worked well this week in pursuit of your goals?

AE

CE

CD

WC

48 | THE STUDY ABROAD JOURNAL

WEEKLY REFLECTION

What didn't work? Where did you struggle?

(We've left you space to write, doodle, or even collage below. You're welcome.)

On a scale of 1-10 (10 being amazing, 1 being a root canal), how do you feel this week?

(1) (2) (3) (4) (5) (6) (7) (8) (9) (10)

A journey of observation must leave as much as possible to chance.
Random movement is the best plan for maximum observation.

— Tahir Shah

Good morning!

WHAT ARE YOU MOST GRATEFUL FOR TODAY?

What's on the agenda for today?

1.
2.
3.

Good evening!
What will you remember most about today?

What actions did you take to meet your goals today?

——— • ——— • ———
DATE

Travel, in the younger sort, is a part of
education, in the elder, a part of experience.

— *Francis Bacon*

Good morning!

WHAT ARE YOU MOST GRATEFUL FOR TODAY?

What's on the agenda for today?

① ....
② ....
③ ....

Good evening!
What will you remember most about today?

What actions did you take to meet your goals today?

If you wish to travel far and fast, travel light. Take off all your envies, jealousies, unforgiveness, selfishness, and fears.

— *Cesar Pavese*

Good morning!

WHAT ARE YOU MOST GRATEFUL FOR TODAY?

What's on the agenda for today?

① ....

② ....

③ ....

Good evening!
What will you remember most about today?

....

....

....

What actions did you take to meet your goals today?

....

....

....

———— • ———— • ————

DATE

We travel, some of us forever, to seek
other places, other lives, other souls.

— *Anais Nin*

Good morning!

WHAT ARE YOU MOST GRATEFUL FOR TODAY?

What's on the agenda for today?

1. ....
2. ....
3. ....

Good evening!
What will you remember most about today?

....
....
....

What actions did you take to meet your goals today?

....
....
....

*Everything I was I carry with me, everything
I will be lies waiting on the road ahead.*

— *Mia Jian*

Good morning!

WHAT ARE YOU MOST GRATEFUL FOR TODAY?

What's on the agenda for today?

① ....

② ....

③ ....

Good evening!
What will you remember most about today?

What actions did you take to meet your goals today?

———— • ———— • ————
DATE

Do not follow where the path may lead. Go
instead where there is no path and leave a trail.

— *Ralph Waldo Emerson*

Good morning!

WHAT ARE YOU MOST GRATEFUL FOR TODAY?

What's on the agenda for today?

1. _____
2. _____
3. _____

Good evening!
What will you remember most about today?

_____
_____
_____

What actions did you take to meet your goals today?

_____
_____
_____

DATE

The more side roads you stop to explore, the less likely that life will pass you by.

— Robert Brault

Good morning!

WHAT ARE YOU MOST GRATEFUL FOR TODAY?

What's on the agenda for today?

1.
2.
3.

Good evening!
What will you remember most about today?

What actions did you take to meet your goals today?

WEEKLY REFLECTION //

What amazing things happened this week?

What will you remember most about this week?

What goals did you work toward this week?

What worked well this week in pursuit of your goals?

AE

CE

CD

WC

WEEKLY REFLECTION

What didn't work? Where did you struggle?
(We've left you space to write, doodle, or even collage below. You're welcome.)

On a scale of 1-10 (10 being amazing, 1 being a root canal), how do you feel this week?

(1) (2) (3) (4) (5) (6) (7) (8) (9) (10)

——— • ——— • ———
DATE

Travel is fatal to prejudice, bigotry,
and narrow-mindedness.

— Mark Twain

Good morning!

WHAT ARE YOU MOST GRATEFUL FOR TODAY?

What's on the agenda for today?

1
2
3

Good evening!
What will you remember most about today?

What actions did you take to meet your goals today?

—— • —— • ——

DATE

*Never hesitate to go far away, beyond all seas,
all frontiers, all countries, all beliefs.*

— *Amin Maalouf*

Good morning!

WHAT ARE YOU MOST GRATEFUL FOR TODAY?

What's on the agenda for today?

1. ....
2. ....
3. ....

Good evening!
What will you remember most about today?

....

....

....

What actions did you take to meet your goals today?

....

....

....

Two roads diverged in a wood and I—
I took the one less travelled by.

— Robert Frost

Good morning!

WHAT ARE YOU MOST GRATEFUL FOR TODAY?

What's on the agenda for today?

1.
2.
3.

Good evening!
What will you remember most about today?

What actions did you take to meet your goals today?

———— • ———— • ————
DATE

I haven't been everywhere,
but it's on my list.

— Susan Sontag

Good morning!

WHAT ARE YOU MOST GRATEFUL FOR TODAY?

What's on the agenda for today?

1.
2.
3.

Good evening!
What will you remember most about today?

What actions did you take to meet your goals today?

Every dreamer knows that it is entirely possible to be homesick for a place you've never been to, perhaps more homesick than for familiar ground.

— Judith Thurman

Good morning!

WHAT ARE YOU MOST GRATEFUL FOR TODAY?

What's on the agenda for today?

(1) _____

(2) _____

(3) _____

Good evening!
What will you remember most about today?

_____

_____

_____

What actions did you take to meet your goals today?

_____

_____

_____

—— · —— · ——
DATE

Because in the end, you won't remember the time you spent working in the office or mowing your lawn. Climb that goddam mountain.

— *Jack Kerouac*

Good morning!

WHAT ARE YOU MOST GRATEFUL FOR TODAY?

What's on the agenda for today?

1. ....
2. ....
3. ....

Good evening!
What will you remember most about today?

....

....

....

What actions did you take to meet your goals today?

....

....

....

DATE

For my part, I travel not to go anywhere, but to go. I travel for travel's sake. The great affair is to move.

— *Robert Louis Stevenson*

Good morning!

WHAT ARE YOU MOST GRATEFUL FOR TODAY?

What's on the agenda for today?

① ....
② ....
③ ....

Good evening!
What will you remember most about today?

What actions did you take to meet your goals today?

THOUGHTS & REFLECTIONS

WEEKLY REFLECTION //

What amazing things happened this week?

What will you remember most about this week?

What goals did you work toward this week?

What worked well this week in pursuit of your goals?

AE

CE

CD

WC

WEEKLY REFLECTION

What didn't work? Where did you struggle?
(We've left you space to write, doodle, or even collage below. You're welcome.)

On a scale of 1-10 (10 being amazing, 1 being a root canal), how do you feel this week?

(1) (2) (3) (4) (5) (6) (7) (8) (9) (10)

*Travel changes you. As you move through this life...you have marks
behind, however small, and in return, life and travel leaves marks on you.*

— Anthony Bourdain

Good morning!

WHAT ARE YOU MOST GRATEFUL FOR TODAY?

What's on the agenda for today?

① ....

② ....

③ ....

Good evening!
What will you remember most about today?

....

....

....

What actions did you take to meet your goals today?

....

....

....

————— • ————— • —————

DATE

One's destination is never a place,
but a new way of seeing things.

— Henry Miller

Good morning!

WHAT ARE YOU MOST GRATEFUL FOR TODAY?

What's on the agenda for today?

① ....
② ....
③ ....

Good evening!
What will you remember most about today?

....

....

....

What actions did you take to meet your goals today?

....

....

....

You can handle just about anything that comes at you out on the road with a believable grin, common sense and whisky.

— Billy Murray

Good morning!

WHAT ARE YOU MOST GRATEFUL FOR TODAY?

What's on the agenda for today?

1.
2.
3.

Good evening!
What will you remember most about today?

What actions did you take to meet your goals today?

——— • ——— • ———
DATE

Never to go on trips with
anyone you do not love.

— *Ernest Hemingway*

Good morning!

WHAT ARE YOU MOST GRATEFUL FOR TODAY?

What's on the agenda for today?

1.
2.
3.

Good evening!
What will you remember most about today?

What actions did you take to meet your goals today?

Travelling-to-a-place energy and living-in-a-place
energy are two fundamentally different energies.

— *Elizabeth Gilbert*

Good morning!

WHAT ARE YOU MOST GRATEFUL FOR TODAY?

What's on the agenda for today?

1
2
3

Good evening!
What will you remember most about today?

What actions did you take to meet your goals today?

———— • ———— • ————

DATE

It sounds so far away and different. I like
different places. I like any places that isn't here.

— *Edna Ferber*

Good morning!

WHAT ARE YOU MOST GRATEFUL FOR TODAY?

What's on the agenda for today?

1. ....
2. ....
3. ....

Good evening!
What will you remember most about today?

....

....

What actions did you take to meet your goals today?

....

....

....

———— • ———— • ————

DATE

Too often travel, instead of broadening the
mind, merely lengthens the conversation.

— *Elizabeth Drew*

Good morning!

WHAT ARE YOU MOST GRATEFUL FOR TODAY?

What's on the agenda for today?

1
2
3

Good evening!
What will you remember most about today?

What actions did you take to meet your goals today?

WEEKLY REFLECTION //

week of

What amazing things happened this week?

What will you remember most about this week?

What goals did you work toward this week?

What worked well this week in pursuit of your goals?

AE

CE

CD

WC

WEEKLY REFLECTION

What didn't work? Where did you struggle?

(We've left you space to write, doodle, or even collage below. You're welcome.)

On a scale of 1-10 (10 being amazing, 1 being a root canal), how do you feel this week?

① ② ③ ④ ⑤ ⑥ ⑦ ⑧ ⑨ ⑩

A mind that is stretch by a new experience
can never go back to its old dimensions.

— Oliver Wendell Holmes

Good morning!

WHAT ARE YOU MOST GRATEFUL FOR TODAY?

What's on the agenda for today?

1.
2.
3.

Good evening!
What will you remember most about today?

What actions did you take to meet your goals today?

———— • ———— • ————

DATE

Life begins at the end of
your comfort zone.

— *Neale Donald Walsch*

Good morning!

WHAT ARE YOU MOST GRATEFUL FOR TODAY?

What's on the agenda for today?

(1) _____
(2) _____
(3) _____

Good evening!
What will you remember most about today?

_____

_____

_____

What actions did you take to meet your goals today?

_____

_____

_____

*The world is a book, and those who
do not travel read only a page.*

— Saint Augustine

Good morning!

WHAT ARE YOU MOST GRATEFUL FOR TODAY?

What's on the agenda for today?

1.
2.
3.

Good evening!
What will you remember most about today?

What actions did you take to meet your goals today?

———— • ———— • ————

DATE

*Every day is a journey, and
the journey itself is home.*

— *Matsuo Basho*

Good morning!

WHAT ARE YOU MOST GRATEFUL FOR TODAY?

What's on the agenda for today?

1.
2.
3.

Good evening!
What will you remember most about today?

What actions did you take to meet your goals today?

———— • ———— • ————
DATE

We are all travelers in the wilderness of this world, and
the best we can find in our travels is an honest friend.

— Robert Louis Stevenson

Good morning!

WHAT ARE YOU MOST GRATEFUL FOR TODAY?

What's on the agenda for today?

① _____
② _____
③ _____

Good evening!
What will you remember most about today?

_____
_____
_____

What actions did you take to meet your goals today?

_____
_____
_____

———— • ———— • ————
DATE

*Travel is very subjective. What one
person loves, another loathes.*

— *Robin Leach*

Good morning!

WHAT ARE YOU MOST GRATEFUL FOR TODAY?

What's on the agenda for today?

1. ....
2. ....
3. ....

Good evening!
What will you remember most about today?

....

....

....

What actions did you take to meet your goals today?

....

....

....

— • — • —

DATE

I am not a great cook, I am not a great artist, but I love art, and I love food, so I am the perfect traveller.

— Michael Palin

Good morning!

WHAT ARE YOU MOST GRATEFUL FOR TODAY?

What's on the agenda for today?

1.
2.
3.

Good evening!
What will you remember most about today?

What actions did you take to meet your goals today?

THOUGHTS & REFLECTIONS

WEEKLY REFLECTION //

week of

What amazing things happened this week?

What will you remember most about this week?

What goals did you work toward this week?

What worked well this week in pursuit of your goals?

AE

CE

CD

WC

WEEKLY REFLECTION

What didn't work? Where did you struggle?
(We've left you space to write, doodle, or even collage below. You're welcome.)

On a scale of 1-10 (10 being amazing, 1 being a root canal), how do you feel this week?

(1) (2) (3) (4) (5) (6) (7) (8) (9) (10)

You know more of a road by having traveled it than by
all the conjectures and descriptions in the world.

— *William Hazlitt*

Good morning!

WHAT ARE YOU MOST GRATEFUL FOR TODAY?

What's on the agenda for today?

1.
2.
3.

Good evening!
What will you remember most about today?

What actions did you take to meet your goals today?

——— · ——— ·

DATE

Certainly, travel is more than the seeing of sights; it is a change
that goes on, deep and permanent, in the ideas of living.

— Mary Ritter Beard

Good morning!

WHAT ARE YOU MOST GRATEFUL FOR TODAY?

What's on the agenda for today?

① ....

② ....

③ ....

Good evening!
What will you remember most about today?

....

....

What actions did you take to meet your goals today?

....

....

....

Certain travelers give the impression that they keep moving because only then do they feel fully alive.

— Ella Maillart

Good morning!

WHAT ARE YOU MOST GRATEFUL FOR TODAY?

What's on the agenda for today?

1.
2.
3.

Good evening!
What will you remember most about today?

What actions did you take to meet your goals today?

———— • ———— • ————
DATE

*How often I found where I should be going
only by setting out for somewhere else.*

— *R. Buckminster Fuller*

Good morning!

WHAT ARE YOU MOST GRATEFUL FOR TODAY?

What's on the agenda for today?

1. _____
2. _____
3. _____

Good evening!
What will you remember most about today?

_____

_____

_____

What actions did you take to meet your goals today?

_____

_____

_____

The use of travelling is to regulate imagination by reality, and instead of thinking how things may be, to see them as they are.

— *Samuel Johnson*

Good morning!

WHAT ARE YOU MOST GRATEFUL FOR TODAY?

What's on the agenda for today?

① ....
② ....
③ ....

Good evening!
What will you remember most about today?

What actions did you take to meet your goals today?

———— • ———— • ————
DATE

Though we travel the world over to find the
beautiful, we must carry it with us or we find it not.

— *Ralph Waldo Emerson*

Good morning!

WHAT ARE YOU MOST GRATEFUL FOR TODAY?

What's on the agenda for today?

① _____

② _____

③ _____

Good evening!
What will you remember most about today?

_____

_____

What actions did you take to meet your goals today?

_____

_____

DATE

No one realizes how beautiful it is to travel until he comes home and rests his head on his old, familiar pillow.

— Lin Yutang

Good morning!

WHAT ARE YOU MOST GRATEFUL FOR TODAY?

What's on the agenda for today?

① _____
② _____
③ _____

Good evening!
What will you remember most about today?

_____
_____
_____

What actions did you take to meet your goals today?

_____
_____
_____

WEEKLY REFLECTION //

week of

What amazing things happened this week?

What will you remember most about this week?

What goals did you work toward this week?

What worked well this week in pursuit of your goals?

AE

CE

CD

WC

WEEKLY REFLECTION

What didn't work? Where did you struggle?
(We've left you space to write, doodle, or even collage below. You're welcome.)

On a scale of 1-10 (10 being amazing, 1 being a root canal), how do you feel this week?

① ② ③ ④ ⑤ ⑥ ⑦ ⑧ ⑨ ⑩

*Half the fun of the travel is
the esthetic of lostness.*

— Ray Bradbury

Good morning!

WHAT ARE YOU MOST GRATEFUL FOR TODAY?

What's on the agenda for today?

1.
2.
3.

Good evening!
What will you remember most about today?

What actions did you take to meet your goals today?

—— • —— • ——

DATE

Not till we are lost do we
begin to find ourselves.

— *Ralph Waldo Emerson*

Good morning!

WHAT ARE YOU MOST GRATEFUL FOR TODAY?

What's on the agenda for today?

1. ....
2. ....
3. ....

Good evening!
What will you remember most about today?

_____

_____

_____

What actions did you take to meet your goals today?

_____

_____

_____

I heard an airplane passing
overhead. I wished I was on it.

— Charles Bukowsi

Good morning!

WHAT ARE YOU MOST GRATEFUL FOR TODAY?

What's on the agenda for today?

① ....
② ....
③ ....

Good evening!
What will you remember most about today?

....

....

....

What actions did you take to meet your goals today?

....

....

....

———— • ———— • ————

DATE

I'm about to cross a time zone, and I feel younger already. If I keep travelling west, maybe I can catch up to the love of my youth.

— *Jarod Kintz*

Good morning!

WHAT ARE YOU MOST GRATEFUL FOR TODAY?

What's on the agenda for today?

1. _____
2. _____
3. _____

Good evening!
What will you remember most about today?

_____

_____

What actions did you take to meet your goals today?

_____

_____

_____

I always wonder why birds stay in the same place when they can fly anywhere on the earth. Then, I ask myself the same question.

— Harun Yahya

Good morning!

WHAT ARE YOU MOST GRATEFUL FOR TODAY?

What's on the agenda for today?

①
②
③

Good evening!
What will you remember most about today?

What actions did you take to meet your goals today?

—— · —— · ——

DATE

Our happiest moments as tourists always seem to come when we stumble upon one thing while in pursuit of something else.

— Lawrence Block

Good morning!

WHAT ARE YOU MOST GRATEFUL FOR TODAY?

What's on the agenda for today?

1. ....

2. ....

3. ....

Good evening!
What will you remember most about today?

....

....

....

What actions did you take to meet your goals today?

....

....

....

DATE

*If you don't know where you're
going, any road will get you there.*

— *Lewis Carroll*

Good morning!

WHAT ARE YOU MOST GRATEFUL FOR TODAY?

What's on the agenda for today?

①
②
③

Good evening!
What will you remember most about today?

What actions did you take to meet your goals today?

THOUGHTS & REFLECTIONS

WEEKLY REFLECTION //

week of

What amazing things happened this week?

What will you remember most about this week?

What goals did you work toward this week?

What worked well this week in pursuit of your goals?

AE

CE

CD

WC

WEEKLY REFLECTION

What didn't work? Where did you struggle?

(We've left you space to write, doodle, or even collage below. You're welcome.)

On a scale of 1-10 (10 being amazing, 1 being a root canal), how do you feel this week?

① ② ③ ④ ⑤ ⑥ ⑦ ⑧ ⑨ ⑩

*I must be a mermaid. I have no fear of
depths and a greater fear of shallow living.*

— Anais Nin

Good morning!

WHAT ARE YOU MOST GRATEFUL FOR TODAY?

What's on the agenda for today?

1.
2.
3.

Good evening!
What will you remember most about today?

What actions did you take to meet your goals today?

———— · ———— · ————
DATE

Tourists don't know where they've been,
travellers don't know where they're going.

— *Paul Theroux*

Good morning!

WHAT ARE YOU MOST GRATEFUL FOR TODAY?

What's on the agenda for today?

1.
2.
3.

Good evening!
What will you remember most about today?

What actions did you take to meet your goals today?

Instead of bringing back 1600 plants, we might return from our journeys with a collection of small unfeted but life-changing thoughts.

— Alain de Botton

Good morning!

WHAT ARE YOU MOST GRATEFUL FOR TODAY?

What's on the agenda for today?

(1) _____

(2) _____

(3) _____

Good evening!
What will you remember most about today?

_____

_____

_____

What actions did you take to meet your goals today?

_____

_____

_____

———— • ———— • ————

DATE

You can't understand a city without
using its public transportation system.

— *Erol Ozan*

Good morning!

WHAT ARE YOU MOST GRATEFUL FOR TODAY?

What's on the agenda for today?

① _____

② _____

③ _____

Good evening!
What will you remember most about today?

_____

_____

_____

What actions did you take to meet your goals today?

_____

_____

_____

*One thing that I love about travelling is feeling
disoriented and removed from my comfort zone.*

— *Sarah Glidden*

Good morning!

WHAT ARE YOU MOST GRATEFUL FOR TODAY?

What's on the agenda for today?

1
2
3

Good evening!
What will you remember most about today?

What actions did you take to meet your goals today?

—— • —— • ——
DATE

A person does not grow from the ground like a vine or tree, one is not part of a plot of land. Mankind has legs so it can wander.

— *Roman Payne*

Good morning!

WHAT ARE YOU MOST GRATEFUL FOR TODAY?

What's on the agenda for today?

1. ....
2. ....
3. ....

Good evening!
What will you remember most about today?

....

....

....

What actions did you take to meet your goals today?

....

....

....

— • — • — •

DATE

Rome is the city of echoes, the city of illusions, and the city of yearning.

— *Giotto di Bondone*

Good morning!

WHAT ARE YOU MOST GRATEFUL FOR TODAY?

What's on the agenda for today?

① ....

② ....

③ ....

Good evening!
What will you remember most about today?

What actions did you take to meet your goals today?

WEEKLY REFLECTION //

week of

What amazing things happened this week?

What will you remember most about this week?

What goals did you work toward this week?

What worked well this week in pursuit of your goals?

AE

CE

CD

WC

WEEKLY REFLECTION

What didn't work? Where did you struggle?

(We've left you space to write, doodle, or even collage below. You're welcome.)

On a scale of 1-10 (10 being amazing, 1 being a root canal), how do you feel this week?

① ② ③ ④ ⑤ ⑥ ⑦ ⑧ ⑨ ⑩

" *Believe you can and you're halfway there.* "

—**Theodore Roosevelt**

———— • ———— • ————
DATE

Okay! You've made it to the halfway point of your program! Congratulations! Now it's time to assess, reflect, adjust your goals, and make a plan for the second half.

How do you feel about your experience so far? Why? Focus on YOUR efforts to make it a great experience (not necessarily how the program was run by others).

On which goal were you especially productive so far? Why?

What are three areas where you can improve in the second half of your program?

1.
2.
3.

——— • ——— • ———

DATE

Revisit your program goals on page 26.

AE **Academic Engagement Goal**

What did you do?

1.
2.
3.

What did you learn?

1.
2.
3.

What surprised you? The good, the bad, the fugly.

What skills have you acquired? These can be hard or soft skills from technical to communication.

1.
2.
3.

How have your opinions on this area evolved?

Does this goal still work for you? If not, what's a better goal?

—— • —— • ——
DATE

CE Cultural Exploration Goal

What did you do?
1.
2.
3.

What did you learn?
1.
2.
3.

What surprised you? The good, the bad, the fugly.

What skills have you acquired? These can be hard or soft skills from technical to communication.
1.
2.
3.

How have your opinions on this area evolved?

Does this goal still work for you? If not, what's a better goal?

—— • —— • ——

DATE

Revisit your program goals on page 26.

CD **Career Development Goal**

What did you do?

① ....

② ....

③ ....

What did you learn?

① ....

② ....

③ ....

What surprised you? The good, the bad, the fugly.

What skills have you acquired? These can be hard or soft skills from technical to communication.

① ....

② ....

③ ....

How have your opinions on this area evolved?

Does this goal still work for you? If not, what's a better goal?

———— • ———— • ————

DATE

WC **Wild Card Goal**

What did you do?

1.

2.

3.

What did you learn?

1.

2.

3.

What surprised you? The good, the bad, the fugly.

What skills have you acquired? These can be hard or soft skills from technical to communication.

1.

2.

3.

How have your opinions on this area evolved?

Does this goal still work for you? If not, what's a better goal?

—— • —— • ——

DATE

We know that not everything you learned and experienced over the last 8 weeks relates to your program goals. In this space, you can write, draw, collage, etc. about your experience. This is your space to be creative and reflect on anything—from the food you ate, the people you met, the places you visited, the conversations you had. It's all fair game. Have at it!

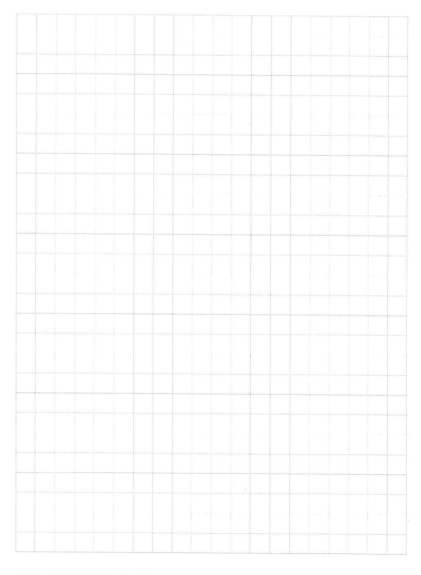

DATE

Great job! You are on your way to study abroad rockstar status. 8 weeks to go!

Own only what you can always carry with you: know languages, know countries, know people. Let your memory be your travel bag.

— Aleksandr Solzhenitsyn

Good morning!

WHAT ARE YOU MOST GRATEFUL FOR TODAY?

What's on the agenda for today?

1.
2.
3.

Good evening!
What will you remember most about today?

What actions did you take to meet your goals today?

———— • ———— • ————
DATE

Travel can be one of the most
rewarding forms of introspection.

— Lawrence Durrell

Good morning!

WHAT ARE YOU MOST GRATEFUL FOR TODAY?

What's on the agenda for today?

1.
2.
3.

Good evening!
What will you remember most about today?

What actions did you take to meet your goals today?

———— • ———— • ————

Every perfect traveler always creates
the country where they travel.

— *Nikos Kazantzakis*

Good morning!

WHAT ARE YOU MOST GRATEFUL FOR TODAY?

What's on the agenda for today?

① ....
② ....
③ ....

Good evening!
What will you remember most about today?

....
....
....

What actions did you take to meet your goals today?

....
....
....

———— • ———— • ————
DATE

I have wandered all my life, and I have also traveled; the difference between the two being this, that we wander for distraction, but we travel for fulfillment.

— Hilaire Belloc

Good morning!

WHAT ARE YOU MOST GRATEFUL FOR TODAY?

What's on the agenda for today?

① _____
② _____
③ _____

Good evening!
What will you remember most about today?

_____
_____
_____

What actions did you take to meet your goals today?

_____
_____
_____
_____

If one had but a single glance to give the world, one should gaze on Istanbul.

— Alphonse de Lamartine

Good morning!

WHAT ARE YOU MOST GRATEFUL FOR TODAY?

What's on the agenda for today?

1.
2.
3.

Good evening!
What will you remember most about today?

What actions did you take to meet your goals today?

———— • ———— • ————

DATE

*We all become great explorers during our first
few days in a new city, or a new love affair.*

— *Mignon McLaughlin*

Good morning!

WHAT ARE YOU MOST GRATEFUL FOR TODAY?

What's on the agenda for today?

1.
2.
3.

Good evening!
What will you remember most about today?

What actions did you take to meet your goals today?

DATE

One travels to run away from routine, that dreadful routine that kills all imagination and all our capacity for enthusiasm.

— *Ella Maillart*

Good morning!

WHAT ARE YOU MOST GRATEFUL FOR TODAY?

What's on the agenda for today?

1
2
3

Good evening!
What will you remember most about today?

What actions did you take to meet your goals today?

THOUGHTS & REFLECTIONS

WEEKLY REFLECTION //

What amazing things happened this week?

What will you remember most about this week?

What goals did you work toward this week?

What worked well this week in pursuit of your goals?

AE

CE

CD

WC

WEEKLY REFLECTION

What didn't work? Where did you struggle?
(We've left you space to write, doodle, or even collage below. You're welcome.)

On a scale of 1-10 (10 being amazing, 1 being a root canal), how do you feel this week?

① ② ③ ④ ⑤ ⑥ ⑦ ⑧ ⑨ ⑩

You develop a sympathy for all
human beings when you travel a lot.

— *Shakuntala Devi*

Good morning!

WHAT ARE YOU MOST GRATEFUL FOR TODAY?

What's on the agenda for today?

1
2
3

Good evening!
What will you remember most about today?

What actions did you take to meet your goals today?

——— · ——— · ———

DATE

Why, I'd like nothing better than to achieve
some bold adventure, worthy of our trip.

— Aristophanes

Good morning!

WHAT ARE YOU MOST GRATEFUL FOR TODAY?

What's on the agenda for today?

① ....

② ....

③ ....

Good evening!
What will you remember most about today?

....

....

....

What actions did you take to meet your goals today?

....

....

....

....

I think a major element of jetlag is psychological.
Nobody ever tells me what time it is at home.

— *David Attenborough*

Good morning!

WHAT ARE YOU MOST GRATEFUL FOR TODAY?

What's on the agenda for today?

1.
2.
3.

Good evening!
What will you remember most about today?

What actions did you take to meet your goals today?

———— • ———— • ————
DATE

The world is a country which nobody ever yet knew by description;
one must travel through it one's self to be acquainted with it.

— Philip Stanhipe, 4th Earl of Chesterfield

Good morning!

WHAT ARE YOU MOST GRATEFUL FOR TODAY?

What's on the agenda for today?

① ....
② ....
③ ....

Good evening!
What will you remember most about today?

....
....

What actions did you take to meet your goals today?

....
....
....

I see my path, but I don't know where it leads. Not knowing where I'm going is what inspires me to travel it.

— Rosalia de Castro

Good morning!

WHAT ARE YOU MOST GRATEFUL FOR TODAY?

What's on the agenda for today?

① ....
② ....
③ ....

Good evening!
What will you remember most about today?

....
....
....

What actions did you take to meet your goals today?

....
....
....

———— · ———— · ————

DATE

There are few places you can find silence. Air
travel could be the last fortress of solitude.

— *Regina Brett*

Good morning!

WHAT ARE YOU MOST GRATEFUL FOR TODAY?

What's on the agenda for today?

1. ....
2. ....
3. ....

Good evening!
What will you remember most about today?

....

....

....

What actions did you take to meet your goals today?

....

....

....

———— • ———— • ————
DATE

I have found adventure in flying, in world travel, in business,
and even close at hand ... Adventure is a state of mind and spirit.

— *Jacqueline Cochran*

Good morning!

WHAT ARE YOU MOST GRATEFUL FOR TODAY?

What's on the agenda for today?

① ....
② ....
③ ....

Good evening!
What will you remember most about today?

....
....
....

What actions did you take to meet your goals today?

....
....
....

week of

What amazing things happened this week?

What will you remember most about this week?

What goals did you work toward this week?

What worked well this week in pursuit of your goals?

AE

CE

CD

WC

WEEKLY REFLECTION

What didn't work? Where did you struggle?
(We've left you space to write, doodle, or even collage below. You're welcome.)

On a scale of 1-10 (10 being amazing, 1 being a root canal), how do you feel this week?

① ② ③ ④ ⑤ ⑥ ⑦ ⑧ ⑨ ⑩

I get a friend to travel with me. I need somebody to bring
me back to who I am. It's hard to be alone.

— Leonardo DiCaprio

Good morning!

WHAT ARE YOU MOST GRATEFUL FOR TODAY?

What's on the agenda for today?

1.
2.
3.

Good evening!
What will you remember most about today?

What actions did you take to meet your goals today?

———— • ———— • ————
DATE

*I enjoy the preparatory elements of travel—packing my bags
and choosing my outfits—but my favorite part is getting there.*

— *Dominic Monaghan*

Good morning!

WHAT ARE YOU MOST GRATEFUL FOR TODAY?

What's on the agenda for today?

1. _____
2. _____
3. _____

Good evening!
What will you remember most about today?

_____
_____
_____

What actions did you take to meet your goals today?

_____
_____
_____

I've met the most interesting people while flying or on a boat. These methods of travel seem to attract the kind of people I want to be with.

— Hedy Lamarr

Good morning!

WHAT ARE YOU MOST GRATEFUL FOR TODAY?

What's on the agenda for today?

1. ....
2. ....
3. ....

Good evening!
What will you remember most about today?

....

....

....

What actions did you take to meet your goals today?

....

....

....

———— • ———— • ————

DATE

You do not travel if you are afraid of the unknown, you travel for the unknown, that reveals you with yourself.

— *Ella Maillart*

Good morning!

WHAT ARE YOU MOST GRATEFUL FOR TODAY?

What's on the agenda for today?

① ....

② ....

③ ....

Good evening!
What will you remember most about today?

....

....

....

What actions did you take to meet your goals today?

....

....

....

....

The whole object of travel is not to set foot on foreign land; it is at last to set foot on one's own country as a foreign land.

— *Gilbert K. Chesterton*

Good morning!

WHAT ARE YOU MOST GRATEFUL FOR TODAY?

What's on the agenda for today?

① _____

② _____

③ _____

Good evening!
What will you remember most about today?

_____

_____

_____

What actions did you take to meet your goals today?

_____

_____

_____

—— • —— • ——
DATE

*I travel light. I think the most important thing is to
be in a good mood and enjoy life, wherever you are.*

— *Diane von Furstenberg*

Good morning!

WHAT ARE YOU MOST GRATEFUL FOR TODAY?

What's on the agenda for today?

1 _____
2 _____
3 _____

Good evening!
What will you remember most about today?

_____
_____
_____

What actions did you take to meet your goals today?

_____
_____
_____

--- • --- • ---

DATE

I mostly like to travel and volunteer because I get
antsy if I stay in my comfort zone for too long.

— Eden Sher

Good morning!

WHAT ARE YOU MOST GRATEFUL FOR TODAY?

What's on the agenda for today?

1. ....
2. ....
3. ....

Good evening!
What will you remember most about today?

....
....
....

What actions did you take to meet your goals today?

....
....
....

WEEKLY REFLECTION //

week of

What amazing things happened this week?

What will you remember most about this week?

What goals did you work toward this week?

What worked well this week in pursuit of your goals?

AE

CE

CD

WC

WEEKLY REFLECTION

What didn't work? Where did you struggle?
(We've left you space to write, doodle, or even collage below. You're welcome.)

On a scale of 1-10 (10 being amazing, 1 being a root canal), how do you feel this week?

① ② ③ ④ ⑤ ⑥ ⑦ ⑧ ⑨ ⑩

It is good to have an end to journey toward;
but it is the journey that matters in the end.

— Ursula K. Le Guin

Good morning!

WHAT ARE YOU MOST GRATEFUL FOR TODAY?

What's on the agenda for today?

① ....
② ....
③ ....

Good evening!
What will you remember most about today?

....

....

....

What actions did you take to meet your goals today?

....

....

....

———— · ———— · ————
DATE

Now more than ever do I realize that I will never be content with a sedentary life, that I will always be haunted by thoughts of a sun-drenched elsewhere.

— *Isabelle Eberhardt*

Good morning!

WHAT ARE YOU MOST GRATEFUL FOR TODAY?

What's on the agenda for today?

1) _____
2) _____
3) _____

Good evening!
What will you remember most about today?

_____
_____
_____

What actions did you take to meet your goals today?

_____
_____
_____

*Every dreamer knows that it is entirely possible to be homesick for a place
you've never been to, perhaps more homesick than for familiar ground.*

— Judith Thurman

Good morning!

WHAT ARE YOU MOST GRATEFUL FOR TODAY?

What's on the agenda for today?

1
2
3

Good evening!
What will you remember most about today?

What actions did you take to meet your goals today?

———— · ———— · ————
DATE

*Travel makes one modest. You see what
a tiny place you occupy in the world.*

— *Gustave Flaubert*

Good morning!

WHAT ARE YOU MOST GRATEFUL FOR TODAY?

What's on the agenda for today?

① ....
② ....
③ ....

Good evening!
What will you remember most about today?

....
....
....

What actions did you take to meet your goals today?

....
....
....

*It can hardly be a coincidence that no language on earth
has ever produced the expression, 'As pretty as an airport.'*

— *Douglas Adams*

Good morning!

WHAT ARE YOU MOST GRATEFUL FOR TODAY?

What's on the agenda for today?

1 ....
2 ....
3

Good evening!
What will you remember most about today?

....

....

....

What actions did you take to meet your goals today?

....

....

....

——— • ——— • ———

DATE

*I am not the same having seen the moon
shine on the other side of the world.*

— *Mary Anne Radmacher*

Good morning!

WHAT ARE YOU MOST GRATEFUL FOR TODAY?

What's on the agenda for today?

1. _____
2. _____
3. _____

Good evening!
What will you remember most about today?

_____

_____

_____

What actions did you take to meet your goals today?

_____

_____

_____

_____

———— • ———— • ————
DATE

*I wandered everywhere, through cities and countries
wide. And everywhere I went, the world was on my side.*

— *Roman Payne*

Good morning!

WHAT ARE YOU MOST GRATEFUL FOR TODAY?

What's on the agenda for today?

① ....
② ....
③ ....

Good evening!
What will you remember most about today?

....
....
....

What actions did you take to meet your goals today?

....
....
....

WEEKLY REFLECTION //

What amazing things happened this week?

What will you remember most about this week?

What goals did you work toward this week?

What worked well this week in pursuit of your goals?

AE

CE

CD

WC

WEEKLY REFLECTION

What didn't work? Where did you struggle?
(We've left you space to write, doodle, or even collage below. You're welcome.)

On a scale of 1-10 (10 being amazing, 1 being a root canal), how do you feel this week?

(1) (2) (3) (4) (5) (6) (7) (8) (9) (10)

*If you reject the food, ignore the customs, fear the religion,
and avoid the people, you might better stay home.*

— James A Michener

Good morning!

WHAT ARE YOU MOST GRATEFUL FOR TODAY?

What's on the agenda for today?

① _____

② _____

③ _____

Good evening!
What will you remember most about today?

_____

_____

_____

What actions did you take to meet your goals today?

_____

_____

_____

———— · ———— · ————
DATE

I am not the same having seen the moon
shine on the other side of the world.

— *Mary Anne Radmacher*

Good morning!

WHAT ARE YOU MOST GRATEFUL FOR TODAY?

What's on the agenda for today?

① _____

② _____

③ _____

Good evening!
What will you remember most about today?

_____

_____

_____

What actions did you take to meet your goals today?

_____

_____

_____

_____

See the world. It's more fantastic than any dream made or paid for in factories. Ask for no gurantees, ask for no security.

— Ray Bradbury

Good morning!

WHAT ARE YOU MOST GRATEFUL FOR TODAY?

What's on the agenda for today?

1. ....
2. ....
3. ....

Good evening!
What will you remember most about today?

What actions did you take to meet your goals today?

———— • ———— •

DATE

Travel brings wisdom only to the wise. It
renders the ignorant more ignorant than ever.

— *Joe Abercrombie*

Good morning!

WHAT ARE YOU MOST GRATEFUL FOR TODAY?

What's on the agenda for today?

① ....
② ....
③ ....

Good evening!
What will you remember most about today?

....
....
....

What actions did you take to meet your goals today?

....
....
....

Don't let your luggage define your travels,
each life unravels differently.

— Shane Koyczan

Good morning!

WHAT ARE YOU MOST GRATEFUL FOR TODAY?

What's on the agenda for today?

1.
2.
3.

Good evening!
What will you remember most about today?

What actions did you take to meet your goals today?

———— • ———— • ————
DATE

The farther you go, however, the harder it is to return.
The world has many edges, and it's easy to fall off.

— Anderson Cooper

Good morning!

WHAT ARE YOU MOST GRATEFUL FOR TODAY?

What's on the agenda for today?

1. ....
2. ....
3. ....

Good evening!
What will you remember most about today?

_____

_____

_____

What actions did you take to meet your goals today?

_____

_____

_____

_____

*But do not ask me where I am going, As I travel in this
limitless world, Where every step I take is my home.*

— Dogen

Good morning!

WHAT ARE YOU MOST GRATEFUL FOR TODAY?

What's on the agenda for today?

1. ....
2. ....
3. ....

Good evening!
What will you remember most about today?

....

....

....

What actions did you take to meet your goals today?

....

....

....

THOUGHTS & REFLECTIONS

WEEKLY REFLECTION //

week of

What amazing things happened this week?

What will you remember most about this week?

What goals did you work toward this week?

What worked well this week in pursuit of your goals?

AE

CE

CD

WC

WEEKLY REFLECTION

What didn't work? Where did you struggle?
(We've left you space to write, doodle, or even collage below. You're welcome.)

On a scale of 1-10 (10 being amazing, 1 being a root canal), how do you feel this week?

① ② ③ ④ ⑤ ⑥ ⑦ ⑧ ⑨ ⑩

Once the travel bug bites there is no known antidote, and I know that I shall be happily infected until the end of my life.

— Michael Palin

Good morning!

WHAT ARE YOU MOST GRATEFUL FOR TODAY?

What's on the agenda for today?

1.
2.
3.

Good evening!
What will you remember most about today?

What actions did you take to meet your goals today?

———— • ———— • ————
DATE

*I didn't know that the world could be
so mind-blowingly beautiful.*

— *Justina Chen*

Good morning!

WHAT ARE YOU MOST GRATEFUL FOR TODAY?

What's on the agenda for today?

① ....
② ....
③ ....

Good evening!
What will you remember most about today?

....

....

....

What actions did you take to meet your goals today?

....

....

....

A good traveler leaves no tracks.
Good speech lacks fault-finding.

— Lao Tzu

Good morning!

WHAT ARE YOU MOST GRATEFUL FOR TODAY?

What's on the agenda for today?

1.
2.
3.

Good evening!
What will you remember most about today?

What actions did you take to meet your goals today?

—— • —— • ——

DATE

*It is not the destination where you can end up, but the
mishaps and memories you create along the way.*

— *Penelope Riley*

Good morning!

WHAT ARE YOU MOST GRATEFUL FOR TODAY?

What's on the agenda for today?

① _____
② _____
③ _____

Good evening!
What will you remember most about today?

_____
_____
_____

What actions did you take to meet your goals today?

_____
_____
_____

Through travel, I first became aware of the outside world; it was through travel that I found my own introspective way into becoming a part of it.

— Eudora Welty

Good morning!

WHAT ARE YOU MOST GRATEFUL FOR TODAY?

What's on the agenda for today?

1
2
3

Good evening!
What will you remember most about today?

What actions did you take to meet your goals today?

——— • ——— • ———
DATE

Roam abroad in the world, and take thy fill of its enjoyments before the day shall come when thou must quit it for good.

— *Saadi*

Good morning!

WHAT ARE YOU MOST GRATEFUL FOR TODAY?

What's on the agenda for today?

1. ....
2. ....
3. ....

Good evening!
What will you remember most about today?

....
....
....

What actions did you take to meet your goals today?

....
....
....

————— • ————— • —————
DATE

Traveling outgrows its motives. It soon proves sufficient in itself. You think you are making a trip, but soon it is making you—or unmaking you.

— *Nicolas Bouvier*

Good morning!

WHAT ARE YOU MOST GRATEFUL FOR TODAY?

What's on the agenda for today?

1.
2.
3.

Good evening!
What will you remember most about today?

What actions did you take to meet your goals today?

THOUGHTS & REFLECTIONS

WEEKLY REFLECTION //

What amazing things happened this week?

What will you remember most about this week?

What goals did you work toward this week?

What worked well this week in pursuit of your goals?

AE

CE

CD

WC

WEEKLY REFLECTION

What didn't work? Where did you struggle?
(We've left you space to write, doodle, or even collage below. You're welcome.)

On a scale of 1-10 (10 being amazing, 1 being a root canal), how do you feel this week?

(1) (2) (3) (4) (5) (6) (7) (8) (9) (10)

How you live your life is up to you. You have to go out and grab the world by the horns. Rope it before it ties you down and decides for you.

— *Sarah Reijonen*

Good morning!

WHAT ARE YOU MOST GRATEFUL FOR TODAY?

What's on the agenda for today?

① ....
② ....
③ ....

Good evening!
What will you remember most about today?

....
....
....

What actions did you take to meet your goals today?

....
....
....

——— • ——— • ———
DATE

Writing is an affair of yearning for great
voyages and hauling on frayed ropes.

— Israel Shenker

Good morning!

WHAT ARE YOU MOST GRATEFUL FOR TODAY?

What's on the agenda for today?

① _____

② _____

③ _____

Good evening!
What will you remember most about today?

_____

_____

_____

What actions did you take to meet your goals today?

_____

_____

_____

Maybe you had to leave in order to miss a place; maybe you had to travel to figure out how beloved your starting point was.

— Jodi Picoult

Good morning!

WHAT ARE YOU MOST GRATEFUL FOR TODAY?

What's on the agenda for today?

① ....

② ....

③ ....

Good evening!
What will you remember most about today?

....

....

....

What actions did you take to meet your goals today?

....

....

....

—— • —— • ——
DATE

The saddest journey in the world is the one that follows a precise itinerary. Then, you're not a traveler. You're a [damn] tourist.

— Guillermo del Toro

Good morning!

WHAT ARE YOU MOST GRATEFUL FOR TODAY?

What's on the agenda for today?

① _____

② _____

③ _____

Good evening!
What will you remember most about today?

_____

_____

_____

What actions did you take to meet your goals today?

_____

_____

_____

What is it about maps? I could look at them all day, earnestly studying the names of towns and villages I have never heard of and will never visit ...

— Billy Bryson

Good morning!

WHAT ARE YOU MOST GRATEFUL FOR TODAY?

What's on the agenda for today?

(1) ....

(2) ....

(3) ....

Good evening!
What will you remember most about today?

What actions did you take to meet your goals today?

——— • ——— • ———
DATE

*I knew then that I wanted to go home, but I had no home
to go to—and that is what adventures are all about.*

— *Trina Schart Hyman*

Good morning!

WHAT ARE YOU MOST GRATEFUL FOR TODAY?

What's on the agenda for today?

1. ....
2. ....
3. ....

Good evening!
What will you remember most about today?

....

....

....

What actions did you take to meet your goals today?

....

....

....

—— • —— • ——
DATE

I've come to realize that sometimes, what you love
most is what you have to fight the hardest to keep.

— Kirsten Hubbard

Good morning!

WHAT ARE YOU MOST GRATEFUL FOR TODAY?

What's on the agenda for today?

① ....
② ....
③ ....

Good evening!
What will you remember most about today?

....
....
....

What actions did you take to meet your goals today?

....
....
....

THOUGHTS & REFLECTIONS

WEEKLY REFLECTION //

week of

What amazing things happened this week?

What will you remember most about this week?

What goals did you work toward this week?

What worked well this week in pursuit of your goals?

(AE)

(CE)

(CD)

(WC)

WEEKLY REFLECTION

What didn't work? Where did you struggle?
(We've left you space to write, doodle, or even collage below. You're welcome.)

On a scale of 1-10 (10 being amazing, 1 being a root canal), how do you feel this week?

① ② ③ ④ ⑤ ⑥ ⑦ ⑧ ⑨ ⑩

I probably did too much thinking in India. I blame it on the roads, for they were superb...

— *Robert Edison Fulton Jr.*

Good morning!

WHAT ARE YOU MOST GRATEFUL FOR TODAY?

What's on the agenda for today?

1) ....
2) ....
3) ....

Good evening!
What will you remember most about today?

....

....

....

What actions did you take to meet your goals today?

....

....

....

———— • ———— • ————
DATE

Japan never considers time together as
time wasted. Rather, it is time invested.

— *Donald Richie*

Good morning!

WHAT ARE YOU MOST GRATEFUL FOR TODAY?

What's on the agenda for today?

1) _____
2) _____
3) _____

Good evening!
What will you remember most about today?

_____

_____

_____

What actions did you take to meet your goals today?

_____

_____

_____

Whenever you go on a trip to visit foreign lands or distant places, remember that they are all someone's home and backyard.

— Vera Nazarian

Good morning!

WHAT ARE YOU MOST GRATEFUL FOR TODAY?

What's on the agenda for today?

1
2
3

Good evening!
What will you remember most about today?

What actions did you take to meet your goals today?

—— • —— • ——
DATE

Wish you were here, we can get lost in the
forest together and eat bamboo rice.

— Winna Efendi

Good morning!

WHAT ARE YOU MOST GRATEFUL FOR TODAY?

What's on the agenda for today?

① _____
② _____
③ _____

Good evening!
What will you remember most about today?

_____
_____
_____

What actions did you take to meet your goals today?

_____
_____
_____
_____

Never hesitate to go far away, beyond all
seas, all frontiers, all countries, all beliefs.

— *Amin Maalouf*

Good morning!

WHAT ARE YOU MOST GRATEFUL FOR TODAY?

What's on the agenda for today?

① _____
② _____
③ _____

Good evening!
What will you remember most about today?

_____
_____
_____

What actions did you take to meet your goals today?

_____
_____
_____

———— . ———— . ————
DATE

Here today, up and off to somewhere else tomorrow! Travel, change, interest, excitement! The whole world before you, and a horizon that's always changing!

— *Kenneth Grahame*

Good morning!

WHAT ARE YOU MOST GRATEFUL FOR TODAY?

What's on the agenda for today?

1. _____
2. _____
3. _____

Good evening!
What will you remember most about today?

_____
_____
_____

What actions did you take to meet your goals today?

_____
_____
_____

---•---•---

DATE

Move to a new country and you quickly see that visiting a place as a tourist, and actually moving there for good, are two very different things.

— Tahir Shah

Good morning!

WHAT ARE YOU MOST GRATEFUL FOR TODAY?

What's on the agenda for today?

① ....

② ....

③ ....

Good evening!
What will you remember most about today?

....

....

....

What actions did you take to meet your goals today?

....

....

....

WEEKLY REFLECTION //

week of

What amazing things happened this week?

What will you remember most about this week?

What goals did you work toward this week?

What worked well this week in pursuit of your goals?

AE

CE

CD

WC

WEEKLY REFLECTION

What didn't work? Where did you struggle?

(We've left you space to write, doodle, or even collage below. You're welcome.)

On a scale of 1-10 (10 being amazing, 1 being a root canal), how do you feel this week?

① ② ③ ④ ⑤ ⑥ ⑦ ⑧ ⑨ ⑩

66

Do not go where the path may lead, go instead where there is no path and leave a trail.

99

—Ralph Waldo Emerson

Congratulations! You did it!

Over the past several weeks and months you've embarked on one of the most powerful experiences of your college career (hey, maybe even your life). And now you've got a physical archive of your experience that you can leverage for your future academic, career, and life goals.

Nice job, you!

TAKING STOCK OF YOUR EXPERIENCE

Remember how we made you decide between amazing and a root canal every week? Yeah. Now you're going to plot those numbers on the graph (total 7th grade style) to see how your experience evolved over the course of your program.

WEEK NUMBER

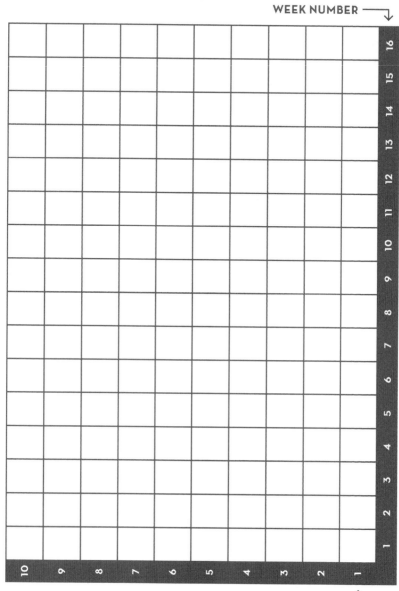

WEEKLY RATING

PROGRAM REFLECTION

It's time to take stock of your entire program abroad and begin to tease out what you learned, what you gained, and how you want to move forward from this experience.

You just graphed the weekly ups and downs of your program. Calculate your average. Is it accurate? How did your ratings fluctuate? What's really going on here...?

How do you feel about your experience? Why? Focus on *your* efforts to make it a great experience (not necessarily how the program was run by others).

What are you most proud of during your time abroad?

What would you change or do differently if you could start all over again?

What will you incorporate into your life back home? This could be activities, ways of thinking, specific skills, etc.

_____

_____

_____

_____

_____

If you could give future study abroad students any advice, what would it be?

_____

_____

_____

_____

_____

What are you most grateful for from your program abroad?

_____

_____

_____

_____

Are you ready for another adventure abroad? Where to next?

_____

_____

_____

_____

It's the moment of truth. It's time to assess your overall progress on each program goal. If you changed goals during your program, that's okay. This is a fluid process that changes and evolves with you. How you decide to reflect on your goal and measure success is up to you.

AE Academic Engagement

Goal: ....

What action items did you take towards this goal?

1. ....

2. ....

3. ....

4. ....

5. ....

Read through your Journal reflections and your progress toward your goals. Are you happy with your efforts? How will you continue striving towards these goals in the future?

....

....

....

What could you have done differently to help you achieve this goal?

....

....

....

What have you learned as it relates to this goal? What skills, connections, knowledge, experiences have you gained as a result of this goal? (Hint: This is the money question. Save this answer for friends, family, future employers, and most importantly, future dates.)

....

....

....

GOAL ASSESSMENT

CE Cultural Exploration

Goal: ....

What action items did you take towards this goal?

1. ....
2. ....
3. ....
4. ....
5. ....

Read through your Journal reflections and your progress toward your goals. Are you happy with your efforts? How will you continue striving towards these goals in the future?

....

....

....

What could you have done differently to help you achieve this goal?

....

....

....

What have you learned as it relates to this goal? What skills, connections, knowledge, experiences have you gained as a result of this goal? (Hint: This is the money question. Save this answer for friends, family, future employers, and most importantly, future dates.)

....

....

....

....

GOAL ASSESSMENT

CD Career Development

Goal: ....

What action items did you take towards this goal?

1. ....
2. ....
3. ....
4. ....
5. ....

Read through your Journal reflections and your progress toward your goals. Are you happy with your efforts? How will you continue striving towards these goals in the future?

....

....

....

What could you have done differently to help you achieve this goal?

....

....

What have you learned as it relates to this goal? What skills, connections, knowledge, experiences have you gained as a result of this goal? (Hint: This is the money question. Save this answer for friends, family, future employers, and most importantly, future dates.)

....

....

....

....

(WC) Wild Card

Goal:

What action items did you take towards this goal?

1.
2.
3.
4.
5.

Read through your Journal reflections and your progress toward your goals. Are you happy with your efforts? How will you continue striving towards these goals in the future?

What could you have done differently to help you achieve this goal?

What have you learned as it relates to this goal? What skills, connections, knowledge, experiences have you gained as a result of this goal? (Hint: This is the money question. Save this answer for friends, family, future employers, and most importantly, future dates.)

THE FINAL STRETCH

It was awesome because ...

This is where we bring home the bacon (or vegan bacon)! One of the most challenging parts of coming home from a meaningful international experience is explaining to everyone just how amazing it really was.

> *You've changed. The way you see the world has changed. What you believe, what you know, what you care about has all been turned on it's head.*

You've changed. The way you see the world has changed. What you believe, what you know, what you care about has all been turned on it's head.

How do you encapsulate that when someone asks, "So, how was it?"

You start by being strategic and knowing your audience. Your friends, your parents, your professors, future employers, random strangers will all expect different types of responses to that ominous question.

To help you out, we've created a "mad libs" style response that you can refine, edit, and reuse as you reflect, synthesize, and make sense of your experience.

We've given you four shots at this so you can create a response based on each goal area you've been working on throughout the program.

Remember this is just the beginning. You'll fine tune these responses and make them your own as you get comfortable with your answers and continue to reflect on your time abroad. This is just the start.

IT WAS AWESOME BECAUSE ...

AE Academic Engagement

My time abroad was awesome! From an academic standpoint I was able

to _____ the _____
   STUDY, RESEARCH, OBSERVE, ENGAGE, INTERVIEW, ETC.   SPECIFIC TOPIC

_____ and understand the

_____ importance of
   HISTORICAL, ECONOMIC, POLITICAL, SOCIAL, ETC.

_____ in _____ .
                                      HOST COUNTRY, CITY, REGION

I'm coming home more _____

and ready to tackle _____
                 SPECIFIC WITH CHALLENGES, ISSUES, OPPORTUNITIES

_____ as I finish up my studies.

CD Career Development

My time abroad was awesome! From a career development standpoint I

was able to _____
          MEET, LEARN, GROW, EXPERIENCE, INTERVIEW, ETC.

more _____
                 SPECIFIC TOPIC

and understand the _____
          ETIQUETTE, PROFESSIONAL LANDSCAPE, CAREER OPTIONS, ETC.

available in _____ . I'm coming home more
          HOST COUNTRY, CITY, REGION

_____ and ready with improved
  CONNECTED, PREPARED, SAVVY, KNOWLEDGEABLE, ETC.

skills in _____
        CROSS-CULTURAL COMMUNICATION, TIME MANAGEMENT, PRIORITIZATION, ETC.

that I'm excited to apply to a future _____ .
                             INTERNSHIP/JOB

CE Cultural Exploration

My time abroad was awesome! From a cultural standpoint I was able to

_____ the _____
MEET, SPEAK WITH, SEE, EXPERIENCE, IMMERSE, ETC.   SOMETHING ABOUT

_____ and understand the
THE CULTURE: LANGUAGE, FOOD, PEOPLE, HISTORY, ETC.

_____ nuances of
COMMUNICATION, HISTORICAL, ECONOMIC, POLITICAL, SOCIAL, ETC.

_____ in _____.
ELEMENTS OF A CULTURAL SOCIETY   HOST COUNTRY, CITY, REGION

I'm coming home more _____

and ready to tackle _____
CHALLENGES, ISSUES, OPPORTUNITIES

_____ as I finish up my studies.

WC Wild Card

My time abroad was awesome! I set a goal for myself to explore

_____
WILD CARD GOAL

with the plan of doing _____
ACTION ITEMS

What I found was _____
NUANCES ABOUT THE LOCAL SCENE

_____ which taught me that

_____ I feel more/less
KEY INSIGHT

_____.
ADVERBS/ADJECTIVES THAT DESCRIBE YOUR PERSONALITY, PERSPECTIVE, ETC.

I can now _____.
INSERT SKILLS HERE

I'm excited to return home and apply what I've learned about

_____ at/with _____
SCHOOL, WORK, INTERNSHIP, FRIENDS, FAMILY, ETC.

THE NEXT LEVEL

Congratulations, you study abroad rockstar!

Now that your program is complete it's time to take things to the next level. Share your experience, story, and feedback with the Study Abroad Journal team. We share profiles of study abroad alumni on our blog and have opportunities for you to become a Journal ambassador on your campus. Let's get started!

Share Your Story

Want to share how the Study Abroad Journal impacted your experience abroad? Visit **www.thestudyabroadjournal.com/story** to submit yours to potentially get featured on our blog.

Provide Feedback

Like you, we're always trying to improve ourselves and the work we do. Have some ideas on how we can make the Journal even better? Share your feedback here: **www.thestudyabroadjournal.com/feedback.**

Become An Ambassador

Do you want to become an advocate for the Study Abroad Journal on your campus? We have awesome opportunities for you to join the team and help us spread the word about the Journal. Learn more at **www.thestudyabroadjournal.com/ambassador**

Connect with us!

Use #abroadjournal and share how you're using your Journal!

@theabroadjournal   /abroadjournal   @abroad_journal

REFERENCES

Gratitude

Emmons, Robert A., and Michael E. McCullough. "Counting blessings versus burdens: an experimental investigation of gratitude and subjective well-being in daily life." Journal of personality and social psychology 84.2 (2003): 377.

Digdon, Nancy, and Amy Koble. "Effects of constructive worry, imagery distraction, and gratitude interventions on sleep quality: A pilot trial." Applied Psychology: Health and Well Being 3.2 (2011): 193-206.

Morning Routines

Vanderkam, Laura. What the Most Successful People Do Before Breakfast: How to Achieve More at Work and at Home. Penguin UK, 2013.

Biss, Renée K., and Lynn Hasher. "Happy as a lark: Morning-type younger and older adults are higher in positive affect." Emotion 12.3 (2012): 437.

Elrod, Hal. The Miracle Morning: The Not-so-obvious Secret Guaranteed to Transform Your Life before 8AM. Print.

Goal Setting

Locke, Edwin A., and Gary P. Latham. "New directions in goal-setting theory."Current directions in psychological science 15.5 (2006): 265-268.

Oettingen, Gabriele. Rethinking positive thinking: Inside the new science of motivation. Current, 2015.

Journaling and Guided Reflection

Brockington, Joseph L., and Margaret D. Wiedenhoeft. "The liberal arts and global citizenship: Fostering intercultural engagement through integrative experiences and structured reflection." The handbook of practice and research in study abroad: Higher education and the quest for global citizenship (2009): 117-132.

Baikie, Karen A., and Kay Wilhelm. "Emotional and physical health benefits of expressive writing." Advances in psychiatric treatment 11.5 (2005): 338-346.

ACKNOWLEDGMENTS

My first adventure abroad was a whirlwind backpacking-style train trip to eight European countries in three weeks. We hopped from country to country not knowing where we would sleep at night with no itinerary. Was I a college student traveling with a bunch of friends? Nope! I was 14 years old with my mom, dad, brother, grandma, and grandpa. That crazy trip planted the seed for all of my study abroad adventures since.

> *Travel is in my blood, and I have my family to thank for it.*

Travel is in my blood, and I have my family to thank for it.

Then, there is Brooke. My partner in crime and companion on the 'study abroad is more than awesome' soapbox. Brooke is the catalyst who takes our conversations and makes them tangible. Without her, this Journal would have remained an idea.

—Natalie

I was 19 the first time I studied abroad. I'll never forget my mom standing at the gate, bawling her eyes out as I boarded my flight to Switzerland where I'd spend the next 6 months. It's to my mom that I give all the credit for inspiring this book. Her unwavering support of all my "crazy" ideas over the years gave me license to pursue my dreams, and indeed, create this journal.

> *Her unwavering support of all my "crazy" ideas over the years gave me license to pursue my dreams*

And of course, I have to thank my amazing co-creator, Natalie. It's incredible what two friends can dream up while sipping craft beer and discussing what makes an epic study abroad experience.

—Brooke

Natalie Garrett

As a life coach, educator, entrepreneur, and lover of learning, Natalie helps individuals take charge of their process and progress to make the most out of any experience. Her career is the epitome of a liberal artist- She's held numerous administrative roles in higher education, been a founding team member at a software startup, and has helped college students do internships all over the world.

Natalie lives in the Los Angeles area, loves swimming and taking her dog Tungsten to the beach, Fridays working from her home office, and exploring the LA's outdoor areas (yes, they do exist) with her husband, Mike. Oh, she also likes journaling.

Connect with Natalie on Instagram @natmcan, Twitter @lifeofnoods, or on her website www.nataliemgarrett.com.

Brooke Roberts

Brooke is passionate about bringing adventure and meaning to all areas of your life. With a background in international education, entrepreneurship, and yoga, she's consulted with individuals, top universities, and growing start-ups to help them level-up their operations, marketing, and presentation to generate a global impact.

Currently based out of Kansas City, she's a big fan of vegetarian BBQ, training for half marathons, sharing stories of other adventurous ones on her podcast, The New Dorothy.

Connect with Brooke on Instagram, Twitter, and Snapchat as @thenewdorothy and on her website www.TheNewDorothy.com